25 to Life

A Guide to Navigating Your Quarter-Life Crisis

Matt Topic

ISBN: 1535021764
ISBN 13: 9781535021760

To Mom & Dad, after all I wouldn't be here without you.

"The woods are lovely, dark and deep,
But I have promises to keep,
And miles to go before I sleep,
And miles to go before I sleep. "

-Robert frost

MATT TOPIC

CONTENTS

Acknowledgments

ACKNOWLEDGMENTS

To my father, my best friend, my mentor, who always pushes me to be the best version of myself.

To my mother, whose love, in silence and words, has paved the way for me.

To my siblings, who I will never tire of fighting with.

To my nieces, who remind me how to smile.

To my family at Holland Avenue and all of my friends who have passed through those doors.

Thank you all, I have nothing but love for all of you.
Cheers to whatever is next.

CHAPTER 1

HAPPY BIRTHDAY

It hits you like a ton of bricks. For a long time, the feeling is neglected, and you don't acknowledge it or pay any attention to it. It may creep up on you from time to time, but you generally just throw it to the side and tell yourself it's a problem for your future self—a lot like a night of binge drinking without considering tomorrow's debilitating hangover. Time goes on. You graduate from university and get that first job or internship, and eventually it just smacks you in the face. You're sitting there in front of your family, your grandma pinching your cheeks, and everything is moving in slow motion. You can hear the faint rhythm of "Happy Birthday to You," but your vision is blurry, and all that comes into focus is the number of candles on the cake.

"Holy shit, I'm turning twenty-five years old."

Your mom is yelling at you to smile while snapping photos as you force a grin through your teeth as the weight of this new existential pain comes crashing down.

All right, so maybe I'm being melodramatic, but it's still a scary moment. I don't think I've ever met a fellow twentysomething who has been particularly excited to turn twenty-five. There has always been some form of angst associated with the number. From my observations, it's become a coming-of-age for self-reflection.

When you break it down, it becomes obvious that turning twenty-five is really the perfect storm for a crisis. The first half of your twenties is finished. There are only five years left until you are thirty (ew, right?), and professionals are telling you these years are the most formative of your life. You start to feel as if you've been wasting them (while wasted) gaining no skills. You look at your résumé and start to think that it is no better than the day you graduated. You've done a lot of partying and sleeping

2

around, and your bank account is just a picture of the Monopoly man with empty pockets.

Take a deep breath because it's going to be OK. Trust me—there are millions of people just like you going through the same thing. Contrary to your mother, the media, and the average number of Instagram likes you get, you are not special in the grand scheme of things. (This isn't a bad thing, and I will address that later.)

So the first step in any recovery program/survival kit is identifying the problem, right? Exhibit A: zombie apocalypse. When the undead are running around eating human brains, the first thing you need to do in order to survive is accept the fact that it's likely the end of the world, and there are brain-dead cannibals sprinting around gunning for your guts. A very quick follow-up to that is to find supplies and take up shelter in a Costco. However, you must first accept reality and come to terms with the fact that, if you want to survive, you are going to have to blast some undead fools. That's right. We are going to treat your quarter-life crisis like a zombie apocalypse.

Say it with me: I'm turning twenty-five, and there is nothing I can do about it. I am a quarter of a century old. I am halfway to fifty. Global warming is for real.

Congratulations! Welcome to the club—you're having a quarter-life crisis. It's all good, and it's better that this happens now than well into your midlife. I feel like a midlife crisis is more expensive than a quarter-life crisis, so kudos to you for being so frugal. So now that you've come to terms with it, let's talk about getting you prepared

It's not just turning twenty-five that has set this all in motion. The birthday cake is more of the straw that breaks the camel's back. There is a slow buildup of this crisis-like powder keg that takes place in your early twenties that isn't being regarded. So it's important to understand what causes this buildup by breaking it down and getting to the bottom of it.

CHAPTER 2

DEVIL IN THE DETAILS

In this chapter I will go after the causes of the crisis and explore some of the lifestyles that contribute to it. Hopefully, you can identify with many of the challenges I bring up.

Social Angst

This is one of the most common causes of a quarter-life crisis; it's fairly general and can be experienced by just about anyone. Social angst comes in many forms; however, you are likely single and caught in some form of social circle purgatory. Half of your friends are married or engaged, are about to pop, are making plans to get pregnant, or at least are making regular plans for team brunches featuring mimosas and some type of frittata you couldn't give a shit about. The other half of your friends spend half the week hungover. They are likely a bit younger than you and wake up with one or all of the following:

- Strangers in their beds
- Not in their own beds
- In the bathroom of a club

This division of your friends isn't helping you; it's just tearing you to either side. On the one hand, you tell yourself that you are getting too old for this, and you need to start taking your life, liver, and finances seriously. On the other hand, you can't see yourself settling down. The closest thing you have to a relationship is how often you hang out with Ben and Jerry, and the only two places you meet potential partners are at a bar and on Tinder. You go to family functions, and your aunt will ask if you are seeing someone as you continue to pile mashed potatoes into your mouth and mutter, "No." You go to weddings, and grandmothers pinch your cheeks and exclaim, "You're next!"—which makes you feel wonderful. If you ever want to get revenge on them for this, when you attend funerals with them, you can say the same thing.

Then you turn twenty-five, and it only gets worse. Should you get a gym membership? Should you do yoga? Maybe a juice cleanse will make you feel better. How about a year abroad in Australia? Oh! You could do CrossFit—definitely do not do CrossFit. This is never the answer.

If this sounds like you, it's all right. Read this handbook; everything is going to be fine.

Searching for Happiness at Work

I have found that this searching-for-happiness-at-work scenario is most common for the rushed graduate. You were a good university student, always wanting to get your hands dirty and never hesitating to volunteer for internships relevant to your field of study. You always spoke about how excited you were to launch into your career when you finished college and how you wanted to get out of the classroom and into the real world. You believed nothing would make you happier than finding a job, falling in love with a profession, making money, and starting your life. It would all start with that internship, right? Right? I mean, of course it would—you would just kill it in your internship, and they would be begging you to stick around, just dying to pay you a salary and give you benefits and a 401(k). I mean, you wouldn't be one of those unemployed graduates—you worked hard!

However, after months of unpaid sixteen-hour days doing nothing related to your career, you really start to question your value within the organization. You realize that the business world is cutthroat, and most people give the least amount of shits about your career aspirations; they just want to get their jobs done. Of course you can always go elsewhere, so you jump from internship to internship, entry level to entry level, unable to ever use any of those handy college credits you spent hours bleeding for. Any theory you ever learned has departed your brain, but you're becoming quite talented at Microsoft Excel. You start to dislike what you do because you believe you should love your work and work for your passion and that somehow the work you are being paid to do will give you some form of fulfillment.

Here is a piece of advice: Take this idea and set it on fire. Let it burn for a while, have a drink, and walk away.

"But what about writers/actors/bloggers/doctors/whatever who follow their passion and love their work?" you ask.

Trust me. They are likely as unhappy and confused as you are, but you just can't see it. There are terrible parts to every job; you will never love all of what you are being paid to do. If you do, then you are a strange specimen who must be examined for scientific research. People have a great way of showing you what they want to show you. If they are posting about how much they love their job on their social media, I would put money on the fact that it is quite the opposite. So if you feel the need to quit what you are doing, or feel as if your life is slipping through your fingers, chill out. You're having a quarter-life crisis. Read this handbook; everything is going to be fine.

The Eternal Student

You probably have a cute Instagram post with this quote: "Education is the key to unlock the golden gate of freedom." You most likely finished your bachelor's degree and decided it wasn't enough. You tell your family and friends that your undergrad education is basically as good as a high school diploma and that you will need to get your master's. You spend the next year carefully crafting a thesis that has a shred of validity in reality and will never be used again. What you will for sure have is fatigue, an empty bank account, an extra five pounds of study weight, and a student loan you are unlikely to ever shake—but that's all fine and good because you will definitely get that employment offer postgraduation, right?

What do you mean they only offered you an internship because you have no work experience? Well, the only logical solution is to go back to school. You decide that you want to become a lawyer (first time you've ever had this urge) because you really enjoyed *Suits*, and that is basically what being a lawyer is like, right? You'll be the next Harvey Specter. After you finish your law degree, you start to consider an MBA, or whatever other piece of education you can think of.

Before I go any further, I don't mean to lump all academics into one pile. You could very well have aspirations of being a professor, or this may be your passion, and I can be very wrong about what I say next.

So if I've offended you, I apologize—suck it up.

Most likely education is comfortable for you. It reminds you of your mother's womb but is much more expensive, and you aren't likely to be completely naked and eating through a belly tube (I said *likely*). There might be something in your head going off, a signal, a questioning of what you've done so far or what you've accomplished. You might have the feeling that some time was wasted in school and that you've taken on too much debt. You see your friends getting into mortgages, contributing to their pensions, and maybe driving new cars, and you start to question whether you should have spent your dollars in a similar way. If any of this rings true, relax, you're having a quarter-life crisis, and everything is going to be fine.

The Bar Star

I didn't choose the server life; the server life chose me. You probably share funny videos with your server friends about shit that servers say. You believe other people can't relate to your daily stressors because they didn't work that double shift with you. What would other people know if they didn't close up the bar with you last night only to open again this morning? Why are you in a bad mood?

Well, because the tip out was crap, and you had a table of people who would just never leave. Duh.

When people ask you what you do, you tell them you serve; however, you follow up by mentioning that it is only temporary. You make mention of the shitty job market and that you are looking for jobs or thinking of starting your own business.

Before I go any further, I don't think there is anything wrong with this path. I am just trying to get you to identify. If this is offending you, you must be a server.

The reality of the situation is that you have been bridging the gap with serving for the better part of a decade; you haven't applied to a single job in a long time; and that back-to-school plan you had, well, it's not happening.

I'm not pointing fingers. The job market does suck, as does being a young graduate these days. The pull of serving is strong, like the dark side. The money is great; it provides you with a social circle that feels like high school or college, but with some creepy old people and a grouchy line cook with a drinking problem. It's easy to fall into because it fits your lifestyle so well. You pick the days you work; your coworkers become your best friends; you party together; it's good money for little work; and at times it can be a blast.

But the problem is that you have stopped learning. You don't feel as if you are growing as a person. You are worried that time is passing too quickly and concerned that you are getting left behind. Everyone you graduated with seems to be getting engaged or promoted or is updating his or her LinkedIn profile to something very annoying, such as publishing a stupid post about productivity: "Ten ways to surprise your boss."

Your résumé is the same as the day you started school. You start to panic, but there is no reason to. Understanding is the first step. You aren't dying— breathe. It's not the end of the world; it's just your quarter-life crisis. As always, everything is going to be fine; read this handbook.

Existential Angst

If you've read the previous paragraphs and related, identified, or found an apt description of yourself, then that's a good thing. It might be a combination of them all—shreds of your identity found across the words I wrote. Hey, you might not identify with any of the items I put on the page. I cannot draw everyone out, and most of my comments are not founded on empirical data but on my own life experiences and observations. I have personally experienced a lot of these feelings and spoken with these people. They have been my friends, girlfriends, acquaintances, classmates, managers, and even my barista at Starbucks.

My own life experiences are woven into this handbook, as I too struggle today with my own crisis—my existential angst fighting to consume me daily. I have found that the only way to beat it is to join it. I acknowledge it and turn it into fuel for my work because, frankly, it's exhausting trying to fight back.

I mention this because it's important for you to know that there are others like you struggling. You aren't alone in this. There are plenty of us out there "suffering" just like you are. I want you to know I have walked in the same or similar shoes, and it's nothing to be ashamed of. You aren't a loser, you aren't unsuccessful, you aren't stupid, and you aren't behind anyone else. You are you,

you are human, and you are awesome.

You must know that reading this book won't magically cure you of anything; I only hope it serves as a guide to better understand what is happening and why. It will contain coping mechanisms, warnings, and other advice that will prepare you for whatever happens next in life. So if you'll have me, let's go on this very short journey together.

MATT TOPIC

CHAPTER 3

SOCIAL MEDIA IS THE THIEF OF JOY

When I speak to older folks about the whole quarter-life crisis thing, they usually just laugh at me. They follow the laughter up with a rant about how it's garbage, and we are just all whiny, materialistic, self-entitled, self-absorbed, and so on.

Well, if I am being honest, a lot of those attributes are true. Our generation, above any other, is obsessed with self-worth, maintenance of our own personal brand, and managing others' opinions of ourselves. Now that is a whole other can of worms I will not crack open because we need to focus on the quarter-life crisis.

Still, my first rebuttal to these baby boomers is that they

are just jealous we are beating them to the whole crisis thing. I mean, they have had to wait until their midlife. This is when their affairs have happened; they bought motorcycles, sold their homes, quit their jobs, and moved to Belize to pursue illustrious careers as street performers by day and flamenco dancers by night. It's been a very strange time in their lives, and all of us who have witnessed it may wonder why that gray-haired man is driving around in a banana-yellow Ford Mustang convertible.

The big takeaway here is that in our lives things are happening a lot faster than in prior generations. I believe that technology has played a large role in this. Let's examine the midlife crisis for a second. (I'm not an expert, but I do have Google.) When you search for causes of the crisis, there are some recurring themes:

- Unhappiness with your life
- Feeling the need for adventure and change
- Questioning your identity and direction in life
- Questioning your relationship with your partner

When we put the quarter-life crisis up against this, we can see a lot of parallels. Looks as if we are beating baby boomers to the punch—suck it Mom and Dad. You guys got great jobs, little debt, and a late crisis. But we totally take the cake—you left us global warming, a terrible job market, and a ton of debt. At least we get our life crisis earlier. Small victories, my friends, small victories.

So why are these crises taking place? Likely not global warming, so let's point the finger at social media. I think our smartphones are slowly causing personal deterioration and are the root of our generational plague. Stay with me for a second.

We have our phones within arm's reach almost twenty-four hours a day: the ultimate companions. They sleep next to us and keep us entertained while we are waiting in line at the store, and we all know we are scrolling while pooping. We spend more time with our phones than with our family and partners, so it's only natural that they have an impact on our lives, right? We are what we eat, and these phones are a transmission device for social media—and believe you me we are gobbling that shit up.

There is an old adage that goes like this: "Comparison is the thief of joy." So I'm reinventing that to reflect the title of this chapter: "Social media is the thief of joy."

Social media is a great tool; don't get me wrong. It's a way to connect and to share and a way to experience the lives of your friends and family who aren't always as close as you'd like them to be. You can express yourself, discover new passions and artists, even fall in love and meet someone special. The intent of social media—connecting us—is a beautiful thing. But not everything is always used for its original intention. (Viagra is a case in point.)

Social media has become a thing of insecurity: building your own brand, comparing yourself, impressing others, and measuring your self-worth on likes, follows, shares, and comments. Posts get deleted on Instagram that don't gain more than eleven likes. Never will the light of day be shone upon the hundreds of unpublished bathroom selfies you and your friends took at the club last night. You create this version of yourself that isn't reality; it's tailored, artificial, and not your true identity.

Our social media pages have also become platforms to highlight our lives, showing the rest of the world only the best parts of our existence. There isn't anything really wrong with this, but those of us looking at your posts aren't digesting the content in the right way. We start to lose our ability to separate reality from social media. We fail to tell the difference between highlights and actuality. The startling truth is that there are 365 days in a year, and not every single waking minute can be an adrenaline rush, backpacking in Europe, or a yacht party. For every highlighted life moment on an Instagram feed, there are twenty-three that never even got a chance to see life through Instagram filters. Here are some social media posts about normal, everyday activities:

"Here's a jar of pickles I bought from the supermarket. #cheatday"

"Doing my taxes."

"Spending thirty minutes scrolling through Netflix."

"Plain oatmeal for breakfast! Canned tuna for lunch! #sohealthy"

All right, so maybe there are plenty of people who post about the most mundane tasks in their lives, but they belong in a special category and aren't what we are talking about. The issue is that social media is creating a new unachievable standard for life. Enter highlight-syndrome theory. Social media is essentially a platform to display highlights of other people's lives. So on a daily basis, we are digesting highlights and raising our expectation of what our reality should be. We start to believe that every single event must be new, exciting, and worth documenting.

When reality enters the scene, we are left with a disappointment. This is a big starter for a quarter-life crisis. We are exposed on a daily basis to beautiful people, beautiful places to visit, and beautiful things to buy and own—creating false criteria for ourselves. It's as if people have become walking advertisements. We see posts of Thailand and ask ourselves the question: "When was my last vacation?" Your trip to another city for dinner seems to pale in comparison to the travel blogger you started to follow recently documenting her six-month stint across Europe. This brings us to our first case study!

I happen to know a travel blogger; you might even follow her yourself. For all of the case studies and people I mention throughout these pages, I will not use names—

for their own protection and mostly at their request.
People love to gaze at her photos, read her blogs, and
follow her posts. I've heard others wish for the life she
has. It's even caused young professionals to question their
own careers. These are educated people with well-paying
jobs. These confused people live in wonderful homes,
drive nice cars, and have job security, benefits, and more
than enough to support any form of lifestyle. If they really
wanted to, they could spend their four weeks of vacation
time doing something similar. Nevertheless, they see my
friend and lust for her life.

You would hope this was a temporary sentiment, but it
comes up in conversation often. It impacts their moods,
their purchases, and their relationships. Think about this:
An Instagram page begins to have an effect on emotions
and daily life. This comparison of one person's life to the
highlights of another person's life sucks the beauty of the
follower's life, and this needs to stop. Don't believe me?
Well let me show you the other side.

Let's meet the woman behind the blog. She travels from
city to city, from hostel to hostel. Most days she doesn't
eat because she can't afford it, and sometimes she goes

without even showering properly. She counts every purchase to the penny, and there is little room to go over budget. While she spends most of her day retrieving pictures and crafting stories, the other fourteen hours of her day are spent trying to sell her stories to websites and promoting herself.

In addition, she has taught herself to write boring content to help with a business's Google ranking—boring stuff—and uses this freelance work to fund most of her travels. Most days when we chat, she is exhausted and hungry and sitting in a crowded hostel with twelve other people who come and go at all hours of the night. If she's lucky, her hostel offers a free breakfast, which consists of a bagel and coffee. Mmm, stale bread.

That's what you don't see or read about. You can't see that story through an Instagram post. You don't get to see the hardships she endures or live through the tough moments with her. She would never show you that—her business is built on your believing her life is wonderful, glamorous, and worth leading. If she failed to do this, she wouldn't be doing her job. If this is the type of life you want to lead, and are willing to deal with these risks, I encourage you to follow her path. I wish you all the best in this world. Conversely, if you feel a little uneasy, keep reading.

Now, we examine the life of another friend, a public servant, who admires my friend the travel blogger. She has a lot going for herself. She has an undergraduate degree with a master's for a cherry on top. She works in the public service, in a management function, which is well ahead of the curve for her young age. She speaks three languages, is paid extremely well, and receives full benefits with dental. She drives a brand new car and lives in a beautiful downtown condo, which will become a long-term investment. She has a savings account with enough zeroes that it takes a second to read. Yes, her job can often be boring, but her day starts around nine and almost always ends at five. Her mornings do not consist of trotting down the Champs-Élysées. They involve rush-hour traffic, but at least she can stop at a coffee shop and get whatever she wants without thinking twice. After work, her hours are her own. She has the luxury of time and the money to pursue what she wants.

What's the big difference? Which one is better? Well, that

is not for me to say. This is rather subjective. For some people, the former still excites them; for others, the latter seems delightful. I have friends to whom I have given the dreadful details of the travel blogger's life, and they have still been convinced that hers is the life they want to live. The takeaway here is to remove the comparison—that is what is hurting us the most. There is beauty in all of our lives; we fail to see it when we only compare our complete picture to the highlights of others. We can start being grateful for the awesome things we have and stop believing the only way out is a radical change. Not one of us is immune from the "daily grind"—we all need to eat, just with different diets.

So let's focus on the title of the book: the quarter-life crisis. How does this case study relate? Well, it will show us what happens when someone decides to act on a crisis in the wrong way. My friend the public service worker actually ended up leaving her job. It started innocently: as a leave of absence. The first six months, she was in heaven, and it felt as if it was the best decision she had ever made. This is generally true for most things in life. It can be a new hobby, relationship, or job. For that period of time in the beginning, it is shiny and new, but after some time, that spark begins to fade. Laziness creeps back in, and reality starts to hit home.

She started to miss her routine—her 6:00 a.m. yoga, trips to the gym, and managing a team at her place of work. She missed walking into a coffee shop where everyone knew her name and what she was drinking. She missed her car and the freedom to drive wherever she wanted. Most of all, she missed her family, friends, and the long-term relationship that ended up suffering as a result of her decision. I'm not sitting here telling you that Instagram made her quit her job, but it damn sure played a role.

"So what? Do you want me to delete my Instagram?"

No, dummy, that's not the point I am making. Continue to post your #pumpkinspicelatte or #dudesnightout. Yes, I believe those things are annoying, but it's within your right to do so. The advice I am trying to give here is that you should provide yourself a chance to separate yourself from it. We have to be able to look at these posts and experiences without comparing our lives to theirs. We need to see them for what they are—highlights. You can't let that strip the joy from your own life. Don't let pictures or someone else's highlights take away from the gifts in your life. This is a problem that plagues twentysomethings. As a generation, we need to learn to live and enjoy the moment—we don't always have to record it. Sometimes it's best to just live with the memory rather than trying to figure out who else hashtagged it.

Social media is really an awesome phenomenon, but as I previously mentioned, it wasn't created to make false idols, comparisons, or any of those shallow things. It was meant as a means of communication, connection, sharing, appreciation, and celebration. So what's the solution? Well, it's a multistep process that has worked for me in the past. Here are some tips for the sake of your crisis.

Step One: Take a Break from Social Media

Take some time off, maybe even a month. I know it sounds crazy, but in my experience, it provides perspective. Try to be a little more "in the moment" in your day-to-day life. Don't post, creep, poke, or like anything. Detach a little from your smartphone apps and laptop. When you're bored, alone, or pooping, resist the urge to mindlessly scroll through one of your feeds. Maybe just try being bored in that moment. I know it's crazy, but do whatever you did prior to having a smartphone.

Step Two: Scrub It

Before you start to return to the teat of social media, I recommend a serious scrubbing of the people you follow. Anything negative, or in bad taste, get rid of. If someone promotes vanity, degrades any person or thing, or posts items that make you feel worse about yourself, then unfollow. I don't need to hold your hand here; you know what to do.

Step Three: Appreciate and Separate

Yes, social media is an awesome tool, so let's keep it that way. Yes, it's meant to share highlights and fun happenings with others, but never to assert yourself above anyone else. Remember, reality versus highlight. Separate the two and move forward. Remember, you don't need twenty mirror selfies. Keep those off your phone and the Internet. Social media is not a drug for your self-esteem problem.

So that's a very quick three-step process to start to chip away at this crisis. This isn't the end, though. It's just the start. There are plenty of factors that add to this crazy angst.

CHAPTER 4

NO, YOU AREN'T SPECIAL

Part One: Plenty of Fish in the Sea

So there are a lot of things and people to blame for the whole quarter-life crisis (yourself included). As previously mentioned, our parents think we are self-entitled, are ungrateful, lack morals, have no relationship skills—you name it. I believe all of that isn't true. Some of it, however, is very correct.

When we wonder why, the answer is rather simple. You see, through our entire upbringings as children, we were taught that we were very special people. We were taught to dream big, that we could become whatever we wanted, that we were unique little butterflies, and that no one was like us. Of course this breeds a generation of entitled brats. As a case study to better illustrate my point out of the gate, I'm going to talk about stages of the modern relationship.

I maintain there isn't any quantitative data to prove what I'm saying. I'm not going to shove statistics down your throat because some among you will argue, find holes in my logic, or write about it in an angry post on Facebook. So instead, I'm going to speak based on my observations of social circles of those in my age group. I'm going to talk about what I've seen, what I've talked friends through, and what are some of my own personal experiences.

I've had a lot of people close to me struggle with relationships, both long-term and flings. In all of my "studies," I've observed three types of relationships, so by breaking them down, I will make some broad generalizations about our belief that we are special and how it's parallel to relationships. Here we go. As a formality I will be throwing shitty dates out the window and assuming most people consistently make it past the first few encounters with the wonderful people they meet.

The point of this next set of ramblings is to see if you can align yourself with any of these situations. Maybe you've been in one or two, or seen someone involved in them. If you can relate, we can start the healing together (namaste).

The Fling: One to Three Months

You met at the bar/Tinder/Snapchat/who cares. You have a couple of really fun dates, but during this weird in-between period, you still tell your friends you are single and casually seeing other people: "Oh I'm just dating around, seeing what's out there."

Tangent: "Dating around" has always confused me, but I suppose it's your call if you decide to treat your dating process more like a headhunting position. Anyway, things are going well, the sex is great, you enjoy spending time together, everything is still new and shiny, and your friends don't really know about the new person yet.

This stage lasts about a month. It's after this that the racy Snapchats stop going out to other people you used to hook up with; you stop "dating around." Instead of going out for drinks, or taking some trip to Ikea that looks like a bad version of *(500) Days of Summer*, you spend an awful lot of time watching series after series with your new person on Netflix. But it's still a date because you are both drinking out of the same bottle of Pinot Grigio Your friends start to see you less, and it's starting to get comfortable.

Your friends get a whiff of the person you are seeing; you start to focus on the small things you don't like about the person.

"Oh, she's a vegetarian."

"He plays ultimate Frisbee."

"He brushes with Colgate—ew."

It gets pretty juvenile, and you even begin to complain to your friends about it. Note: When you start talking about your relationship to an audience of people, it's the beginning of the end. I'm not going to tell you what to do, but it's not a good idea to air your dirty laundry with others. You take a good hard look at the situation and decide it is best to move on—that you can do better. You go back to your Snapchat friends, Tinder matches, and one-night stands. You deserve the best, she/he wasn't that great, and you are very special. You let go of anything in the relationship that resembled progress or made you happy and start off in another direction looking for perfection. You deserve perfect—you're special, after all, aren't you?

There's a Drawer of My Things at Your Place: Three to Six Months

In my experience, this is the fork in the road for people. If you can make it to six months, you are doing pretty good, but at our age, it's generally shit or get off the pot. You are either going to continue to see this person or go your own way. If you can hang out with that person and not want to pull your hair out, you have made progress, grasshopper. This is where things get interesting. Your "special friend"—God forbid we call him or her your girlfriend/boyfriend—starts to meet your social circle. They form opinions, and you have opinions of his/her friends. Your friends have likely voiced those opinions to you. (Note: Opinions in terms of your relationship should be like other people's mixtapes—you don't want to hear them.)

Well, if you've listened to these opinions, there's a chance they've gotten into your brain and you've started to question yourself—BAD SIGN. Now you have become infected. The new person has a drawer of shit at your place. It's not like an intimate thing; it just makes sense that the special friend has stuff there—at least that's what you've told yourselves. Those opinions of your friends started small, but they started to get bigger and bigger, and you began to make something out of nothing.

Now things go one of two ways, depending on the kind of person you are. Either at this point you start to explore your options again and begin to drift apart, or you end up sticking together. I won't go much further down the relationship road to avoid ranting, so I will just get to my point.

My point is that in society today, relationships seem to end for no good reason—getting shot down and suffocated before they get a chance to take a breath. Breakup reasons, I've heard, are juvenile, small things, like not liking one of the person's friends, dog, or career. I'm not joking. I have heard the most ridiculous excuses for an exodus from a relationship. So why? Is this new? All right—here is where I throw my mixtape opinion at you and expect you to listen. This is where I tie together the chapter, so buckle up.

We like to think we are special and deserve the perfect relationship. We have created a false image of what we believe we deserve. We think it's possible to attain this level of love because all of the mediums around us tell us that's the case. Social media shows us all the beautiful parts of other relationships. What makes matters worse is that if you don't believe it's working, other people have never been more accessible due to the Internet. A new hookup or date is a text message away, making it easier than ever to get back on your feet because there are plenty of fish in the sea, right?

Before I dig my hole any further, let me make one thing perfectly clear: If your relationship is toxic, abusive, unhealthy—get out. If you aren't growing, dislike the other person, don't want to be around him or her—break it off.

Now, let's move forward.

We tell ourselves white lies, which gives us reasons for

never allowing a partnership to blossom with another person. Instead of working on a relationship, growing with a person, or fighting for something that is worth it, we simply cast it aside and move on.

"I want to focus on my career anyway."

"She didn't get along with my friends."

"I didn't like the way he dressed."

"I'm not really ready for a relationship."

"I don't have the time."

We tell ourselves these reasons, but we know it isn't the case. You may be asking at this point: "What does this weird relationship sorting/advice thing have to do with the title of the book?" Well, here goes nothing.

We treat our lives the same way we treat our relationships. We believe we are entitled; we believe we are special; we believe we are unique sunflowers. The same way we believe our lives are not magnificent enough is the same outlook we have toward our engagements with others. If it isn't perfect, it isn't worth our time. We believe we are entitled to certain privileges, and this simply isn't the case. When this expectation meets reality and isn't fulfilled, we end up with a quarter-life crisis.

It's not our fault either; we are bred into this age of entitlement. As I said, we are brought up to believe we are unique, with unique dreams and aspirations. We have been told we are beautiful in our own way and that the world is our oyster. We are told that if we work hard in school and study, the world will lay itself at our feet. Our moms and dads praise our work as if we were the next coming of Hemingway or Oscar Wilde.

To make us feel even more special, pop culture has taught us that there is a moment where we meet "the one," and we will never have a doubt in our minds. That will be the person, without a doubt, we should spend the rest of our lives with. Our minds should never wander or will never waiver. I watched *The Notebook* with Ryan Gosling once, and I'm still looking for my Rachel McAdams—I dare not tell a girl, "If you're a bird, I'm a bird!"

I hate to break it to you, but the movies aren't reality. The reality of the situation is that relationships are a lot of work—like anything worth having. If it's broken, you work at fixing it, if it's worth it. I was raised under the premise that a relationship is something you have to work at every day, and a lot like life, there are peaks and valleys, not a twenty-four-hour highlight reel. Starting to see the connection? Highlight-syndrome theory bleeds into all parts of our lives. We want gratification, we want happiness, and we want it now, goddamn it.

All of these stories of overnight success and university dropout success stories aren't helping us battle highlight-syndrome theory either. We begin to create a mind-set that it's possible for us as well. Like we can miraculously skip all of the steps and be a happy success story. However, like an Instagram page, there is a lot in these stories we aren't seeing. Facebook took years of hard work before it made a penny; Apple went through ebb and flow. It's all well and great to see Tom Brady sling touchdown passes on Sunday, but what we don't see is his rehearsing that pass a thousand times a day in practice. Not much glamour in those things.

Instead of understanding the process, we get disappointed when we fail, see things at a shallow level, and expect the universe to tilt in our favor, but we are ignoring a very harsh reality I will now share with you. If you wanted to be the next great guitar player, you'd be practicing scales for eight hours a day, not just playing fun songs. If you wanted to be a great actor, you'd spend hours working on your expressions, building and falling into characters, memorizing scripts and monologues, and auditioning till your legs fell off. Malcolm Gladwell in *Outliers* wrote, that it takes ten thousand hours to truly master something. If you broke that down into more relative time, it's about 416 days of twenty-four hours a day.

If you are awake sixteen hours a day and beating on your craft half of those awake hours every day of the week, it would take 3.4 years for you to pile up ten thousand hours to master something. If at any point that amount of work makes you cringe, or you feel dissuaded just by hearing that, do yourself a favor and quit. I don't mean that in a negative way. But think about it. If some words from a joker like me can start to convince you not to do something, you're either extremely impressionable or probably didn't want to do it that much in the first place.

The bottom line here is that you aren't special. You likely won't have a miracle dropped in your lap that takes out all elements of hard work. You're not the greatest thing since sliced bread. There's nothing wrong with not being special, though. You may not be destined to write the next Harry Potter book, star in a Martin Scorsese film, or win the next Super Bowl, but that's fine. In fact, it's awesome; it's great. Because the sooner you can accept all of those things, the happier you will be.

So what does being special, relationships, and the Super Bowl all have to do with this book? Well, the point I am making (starting with relationships) is that life is found in the process of developing and working on that relationship. The special part is all the little things—not only the highlights. So in terms of the process of dealing with your quarter-life crisis, we are making headway. We've learned that we are not special. Now we have to see what happens when we have great expectations that don't match reality.

Part Two: Not-So-Great Expectations

I think there is something to be said for setting goals. When done right, goals are healthy, constructive, and give us something to work toward. As soon as we set a goal, we begin to unconsciously work toward it. When we break it out into short-, mid-, and long-term goals, we give our minds something to focus on, and the goal brings us back to earth when we begin to run off the rails. However, expecting to be famous, or wanting to be the next LeBron James, isn't really a goal—it's more of a grand expectation that will ultimately lead to a letdown.

Why's that? Well, let's examine your college education for a second. Getting a job after college can be a goal (and something to work toward), but it isn't very specific, and it sounds more like an expectation: "Because I went to postsecondary school, I will get a job."

It doesn't help that throughout your career as a student you are being told that once you leave that money-sucking institution known as a university, you will be offered a well-paying position. So you work through your university career with this expectation that has been created. You don't have any goals to achieve it; you just go through the movements of being a student with the belief that at the end of this there will be a job offer waiting for you. You might even start to fantasize a little bit, perhaps envisioning a life where you have your own place, a nice car, and the ability to travel more.

You continue to load this expectation more and more. The more weight it carries, the more it will hurt when the expectation isn't met. The day finally comes when you walk across that stage wearing a funny hat and holding a piece of paper in your hand. Your parents clap in the audience, but you can't wait for this ceremony to be done because you are very hungover and couldn't care less who is magna cum laude.

But really, who cares? You have your piece of paper. You send that beautiful résumé out into the world and— nothing. Not a callback, not an interview, not anything. These expectations you've built are like a barbell. You've slapped six hundred pounds on it, and now you are going to try to lift it. Well, you're going to have a bad time.

Remember when we talked about reality smashing headfirst into expectations? Well, here it comes. You didn't get a job, and they want someone with more experience than you. The fact is you will have a hard time getting any job, and it's not your fault. It's the fault of a terrible system in which the upcoming generation is getting taken advantage of. All of the "entry-level" positions require you to have one to three years of working experience, but when were you supposed to get that? In between working full time at a Starbucks and going to school? That car you picked out and priced isn't going to happen. That apartment you dreamed of is going to stay a dream for now. Now that reality has set in, we are just fueling the quarter-life-crisis fire. People tell you just to get any job, but let's face it, you have a four-year degree, and you're above working at Starbucks! (This is very wrong; you aren't above anything.)

You may tell me that you didn't just have expectations; you worked hard and got good grades. Sorry, kid, not enough. You needed to have a goal. You needed to have a list of companies you wanted to work for and strategically network with, and you needed to create a portfolio of work while you were in school to gain that entry-level experience, so when the time came, you were prepared. But you didn't do that, and it's not your fault. No one in school prepares you for that; no professor sits you down and gives you the hard truth. The institution you're attending is just greedy and only cares about getting your money every year and screwing you over wherever it gets the opportunity.

I never had a class on writing a résumé, and I was never lectured on how to write a proper cover letter, how to stand out to employers, or what type of experience I would need. Instead I fended for myself, googled around, and tried to figure it out. I sit around with a handful of theories to use on communication but nowhere to apply them. I'm twenty thousand dollars in debt and don't have a real means, other than minimum-wage work, to pay it off.

How familiar does this story sound to you? Frankly, it's bullshit. You know that they will tell you the solution is an internship, an unpaid internship. People will tell you that's the way to get entry-level experience, network within the organization—it's a great way to get your foot in the door.

There are a couple of problems with unpaid internships, starting with exploitation. It's as if the current structure is just meant to burn us. Here's a grand idea for you—

remember that expectation you had that once you finished school you'd get a full-time job in order to offset all of that massive debt you once had? Well, we know now that it's bullshit, so we'll create a new expectation for you. Take this unpaid slave-labor job as a shot at getting full-time work. Wow, that makes a lot of sense. So you're saying I could be working a service job making money, actually reducing my overall debt, or I could be working for free.

Here's the problem with these internships. Often these were fully paid positions that were cut back in order to save money, and managers realized they could get kids like you to do it for free. What's the greatest thing of all? Once these internships are all said and done, it's still a gamble of whether or not you get that job—doesn't matter how many hours you bled. If there are no jobs, there are no jobs; this is the reality. The expectation of getting a job post internship? Don't let it hold too much weight.

We have to deal with all of this while trying to figure our own lives out. It's no wonder we have these crises. We have no guidance, no real mentorship, or any other help here. One can say we have our parents, but frankly, and with all due respect, our parents know nothing when it comes to the job market today. They all grew up in an era mostly void of technology, where jobs were generally readily available to them if they had a university degree.

Today, we have to navigate LinkedIn, job boards, making portfolios, and "proving ourselves." All the while you sit there thinking, "Wasn't that four years enough?" Expectations that you were conditioned to create are crushing your reality. But there's hope, right? Look at Mark Zuckerberg and these new tech giants. You're told the world is your oyster, and now is the time of opportunity. Learn to code, create your own app, start your own business, do your own thing.

Here's some more reality for you. We are all not the next creators of something like Facebook; we aren't all meant to change the world on some grand scale. We aren't all CEOs, inventors, or geniuses. Some of us don't have the ideas, capital, or time. Nor are we built the correct way to accomplish this goal. So what do we do? Once again, because these types of expectations are put in place for us and we fall short, it's another blow to us and another weight stacking on top of the others that contribute to the quarter-life crisis.

None of this can really be healthy. The times they are a changing, but it seems nothing is in place to help us change with them. No one ever prepared us for this or could have even expected this rapid change. We are the first to bat on this new school of doing things. I hope that by the time I have children and they grow up, this is all figured out—because right now, it's bogus. It's easy to point the finger at us and call us self-absorbed, entitled, selfish, lazy, and so on. It goes on, and boy, do those comments ever make us feel great. But we have to ask ourselves, and question the finger-pointers, how did we get this way? Did we just decide? Maybe it has something to do with how we were conditioned. Maybe it's how we were brought up, what we were brought up around. Maybe it has something to do with institution. However, there's no point whining and complaining; what's done is done. At this point, all we can do is acknowledge it, learn from it, and help ourselves. We need to make a conscious decision to make a change. That brings us to the next point in this handbook: fear of making decisions.

CHAPTER 5

FEAR OF MAKING DECISIONS

I believe one of the toughest things we have to do is make decisions. I'm not talking about the day-to-day decision-making, so don't go poking holes in my argument by saying, "Oh I decided to take a poop this morning, and that wasn't a hard decision." I am referring to the decisions that have a larger impact on our lives such as what university you attend, what career path you embark upon, or whether to stay in a relationship. These are some tough things to decide.

We human beings are very adept at getting things done when a decision is already made and the path is laid out before us. It gets tricky when you have to make the decision on your own. Big decisions exhaust us, and we often waiver, weighing the pros and cons. We allow our friends and family to give their opinions. Some people make lists, some people jump instinctively, and some flip a coin. However, from my observations, we often don't make a choice at all because of fear.

So we are afraid to make decisions, and this plays a crucial role in the quarter-life crisis. I'll use another case study of a friend of mine.

When we first started communicating, my friend was twenty-five and at a very interesting time in his life. He was an all-star athlete throughout his adolescence and into his college career, and along the way he maintained a solid GPA. His dream was not, however, to become an academic but to be drafted into the NFL. So after college he waited for his name to be called, but it never happened for him. He bounced around on some practice squads for a while, but it never worked out.

He needed to make some money, so he started serving at a restaurant full time. He still trained daily, kept in great football shape, and played in a semicompetitive league to keep his skills and football IQ up. He even tried to work his way into the corporate world with a combination of his good grades and networking, but his job search kept coming up dry. You see, in college he spent all of his days playing football and didn't have time for job placements or extracurricular activities. He had no real working experience.

I need to rant here for a second.

Digression

So he's been beaten a couple of times in life, but as football taught him, it's not about the times you get knocked down; it's how many times you get up. How long are we going to be told that same story? Success is not the number of times life beats you down; it's that last time you get up that counts. Sounds kind of masochistic doesn't it? Is there no nicer way we can put it? It's like saying, "Life sucks, kid. It's going to be terrible, and you are going to lose all the time. And hopefully, you will have the internal strength and willpower to recover so you can lead a good life."

Now, I understand this concept very well. Nothing worth having comes easy, blah blah blah. I won't say anything here that can be said in some Instagram post to someone who went to the gym for the first time. What I will say is why are there are so many obstacles for our youth? The leaders of the future are going through some of the hardest times mentally, and we are just shrugging it off. We are saying that this is just a lazy generation, full of entitlement and everything else I've been speaking about for the last several pages.

But as I said, these conditions are a result of the environment we are being brought up in. Have you ever thought about the amount of fortitude it takes to be beaten time after time, to continually try to reinvent yourself to do something as simple as getting your first job? But I digress.

So my friend and his job search come up dry, so now he has to weigh his options. He has the opportunity to do many things here. He draws up a list:

1. I can wake up every day and burn my ass and train toward competing in football, hoping to make the NFL.

2. I can go back to school for a master's degree in hopes of that increasing my qualifications for full-time work.

3. I can take some time off and travel for a year, explore, find myself, and Zen out.

4. I can continue trying to get a marketing job, work toward internships, and work part time.

5. I can get a serving job to tide me over while I wait for the job market to turn over.

6. One of my fellow teammates has started in real estate; maybe I should give that a shot.

7. I have a college degree, so I could also teach overseas for a year.

8. I have a strong knowledge of fitness and physical health. I could pursue the area of personal training.

Right there, that is eight possibilities for a young man. That wasn't even all of them—I remember receiving this full list from him, and it was pretty lengthy. Some of the items on it were ridiculous, with almost no chance of success. Since I'm not using names, he even considered becoming a YouTube blogger. So with all of these decisions, he faced two main issues. The first was how he created so many. As detailed in previous chapters of the book, we have deemed ourselves special, and to that effect we've decided that there isn't anything we can't do (thanks, generic motivational sports apparel advertisement). This gets into our heads, and we lead ourselves to believe that our world is still an open book at twenty-five. This isn't entirely true. As much as society would like me to believe it, after some time there are certain things I cannot do with my life. I'll name a few: NFL player, PGA pro, world's fastest man, Hollywood actor, president of the United States.

Why? Well, I haven't spent any time on the football field, and I'm twenty-five. With golf I struggle to break a hundred. I haven't ever taken an acting lesson in my life. And I'm not a citizen of the United States.

These may seem like big or unfair examples. But there is a point to be made. It would be very difficult for him to become a YouTube superstar because he has no editing, filming, or writing experience. He could very well use the beautiful resource of the Internet and dedicate a fair amount of his time learning how to use it if he truly wishes to pursue it, but he is much better equipped to act on some of his other possibilities for life. It's like hedging your bets, but for life. So how does my friend's story go? What did he do?

For a while he did nothing. Day in, day out, nothing changed. My friend didn't make a decision for a long time because he was afraid. Afraid of making a decision. We start to worry that we will be unhappy with the outcome, that the path we are about to set foot on is going to be wrong, or that we will regret what we are doing—but what we fail to realize is that this is life. Life is all about walking down the wrong path sometimes, making mistakes, living with the consequences of our actions, and learning and growing from them, and this realization is one of the best aspects about being alive.

We don't see this because we want everything to work out perfectly, just like on social media. The reality is that it will never look like that. It will be full of bumps and mistakes, but those are awesome because you learn from those and grow as a person. I would rather do something and fail rather than live with the thought of "What would have happened if I had done it?"

Instead of pulling the trigger on something, we live our lives in a form of stasis with no growth. Our fear of making decisions only makes our quarter-life crisis worse, because it keeps us in crisis mode longer. Like in a war in which we're deciding to stay put rather than to advance or retreat, we stay in the same situation, when all we need to do is make a decision, live with it and its consequences, and move forward. So did my friend ever come out of this funk?

He and I spoke frequently, and we landed on a couple of options. He mapped out his priorities and realized financial stability took priority, and he wanted to be employed somewhere he felt important. He was fortunate enough not to have accrued any student debt as a result of an athletic scholarship (not everyone is this lucky), but he had little savings. I encouraged my friend to get a job, any job, so as not to leave a gap in his employment history. Nevertheless, he still missed football.

Eventually, my friend would go on to volunteering at his alma mater in training the football team, and he now sits as an assistant coach. Not everyone is this lucky, but because he made a decision, things started to happen for him. He continued to make decisions, and the road before him became more apparent.

I'm not saying it happens this way all the time—but it can. Because he made the choice that he needed to support himself, he fulfilled that need within Maslow's hierarchy (a theory that believes that certain states such as stability must be achieved in order to grow), and he could see that he missed the game of football. He then used his connections to accomplish this goal, and here he sits today, on the outside of his quarter-life crisis.

As I've mentioned, it's not always smooth sailing. We are all not so fortunate to have collegiate connections, athletic scholarships, or other factors that give us an advantage in life. Yet we all have the power to make a choice—any choice—sticking to it, and seeing it through to completion. We reach a critical point in our lives where we just need to decide what it is we want to do. A lot of people get this confused with the common quote that comes from motivational speakers: "Just decide who it is you want to be, what it is you want to do; just make a decision."

I don't agree with this completely. The decision you make now doesn't have to be permanent. It doesn't have to shape the rest of your life. At twenty-five you are only a third of the way through your life, so there's plenty of time to change your mind. Nonetheless, it is important to note one part of that quote. Decide who you want to be. What type of person do you want to be? I think that's the more important decision. That leads us to the next point of this handbook—about building character.

CHAPTER 6

BUT IT BUILDS CHARACTER

When I was a kid, I was a huge fan of the Bill Watterson comic strip *Calvin and Hobbes*. I was obsessed with these books of comics and would rarely travel without one in my backpack. My parents made sure my collection of them was complete, and I made sure I read them cover to cover. They were full of life lessons that would come in handy later on in my life. They would teach me the importance of creativity, imagination, friendship, and never taking anything at face value—the art of skepticism.

A line that always stuck with me was spoken by Calvin's father. It always happened when he would task Calvin with something like shoveling the driveway, and Calvin would complain. His dad would always respond in turn with "but it builds character."

At the time I never understood it, but as I grew older, I began to grasp the concept in a more complete form. As I spoke about in previous chapters, there are many moving pieces in your life—the type of job you want, the person you want to love, the school you want to go to. It's difficult to have control over these, but your character is totally up to you, regardless of outside circumstances. I will speak to both character and your values briefly in this chapter as they relate to the crisis.

Let's start with your values. Believe it or not, your set of values will really drive every decision you ever make without your even being aware of it. If you take the time to learn about yourself, you might find out what exactly these are, and believe you me, it will pay dividends. Your values are what is most important to you in life. It's easier for me to explain by taking you through an exercise.

Let's take ten standard values to start:

1. Health
2. Wealth

3. Prestige

4. Love

5. Education

6. Adventure

7. Family

8. Friends

9. Learning

10. Beauty

Now, you can only pick five from that list. When you've done that, remove two from that list. Those are your top three values. Now, once you have an understanding of those, every time you need to make a decision, you can base it off those values. So if my top three values are health, family, and love, and I have a job offer across the country, but I'd be working long hours, would be taken away from my family, and would have to leave my girlfriend, that decision becomes a no-brainer. Why? Because it doesn't line up with any of my values. This exercise allows us to develop a system that prevents us from making decisions from a shallow perspective and forces us to make them in line with who we are as people.

Our values develop over time but generally never change.

In my experience, if your values don't match up with your partner's, it doesn't always work out between the two of you. Don't believe me? Well, if religion is really important to you and not to your partner, is that a problem? How about if you are very into health and your partner isn't? These might seem obvious to you, but I'm speaking to values at a very macro level. In short, your values are the guiding principles for your life. In terms of a quarter-life crisis, if we begin to understand our values and know what is important to us, the problem of being twenty-five becomes much smaller. We are able to see further ahead and identity if we are truly doing the right things at this moment in time.

So how does character differ from this? While values are the guiding principles for your life, character is the guiding principle for how you behave while walking through life. Character is shown in how we respond to the things that happen to us throughout our day. Didn't get that job offer? Well, did you complain and make excuses, or did you start adjusting your résumé again? Partner break up with you? Did you beg for them to come back, or did you hit the gym?

Values can't really be built and don't change, but like a muscle, you can work on character. You can build character through habits and practice, but the motivation has to be there. If you have a weak character and get blindsided with a quarter-life crisis, it is going to hit you really hard. But if you listen to Calvin's dad and build character, you will be able to work through it. It's built by pushing yourself outside your comfort zone or just by being more aware of others. I won't write an essay on building character 101 because that's a whole book in itself.

The reason I am here (and you are reading) is to guide you through your quarter-life crisis. So now that together we've identified issues and opened wounds a little further, we are going to work on the healing. Step-by-step.

MATT TOPIC

CHAPTER 7

STEP-BY-STEP

Talking about the problem is easy. It's much harder to actually do something about it. Up until now I've just complained about it a lot. You've read the case studies mixed in with my rants and things that rattle my cage. Now it's time to give some guidance. Here comes a dose of reality: You can't beat a quarter-life crisis. There is no antibiotic to take or no liquor strong enough to numb the pain of it (I could be wrong). Like any recovery program, the first step is acceptance.

Step One: Accept the Confusion, Accept the Crisis

"You'll be fine. You're twenty-five. Feeling "unsure" and lost is part of your path. Don't avoid it. See what those feelings are showing you and use it. Take a breath. You'll be OK. Even if you don't feel OK all the time," said comedian Louis C.K.

The first step in beating the crisis is swallowing the pill. The next part is realizing that there is nothing wrong with that. The quote by Louis C.K. does a great job of getting that point across. I could end this step right here, but it wouldn't be like me not to ramble on about something.

I've made this point in smaller ways at previous points in the handbook. We can't fight our situation, so take a break, inhale, and say it with me: "I'm twentysomething, confused, and have no idea with what to do with my life, and that's completely fine." Repeat that a couple of times, and you might even start feeling better.

We have to come to terms with a lot of aspects of our lives. It may sound negative, it may sound pessimistic, but it's necessary and better than spending a whole lot of time in denial. There are certain goals you will never achieve. Certain dreams will never come true. You will likely never catch a touchdown pass from Tom Brady or act alongside George Clooney. The quicker we can accept certain truths about our lives, the happier we will be. If I am saying any of these things and you disagree, then please prove me wrong. Show me that I am incorrect.

This isn't a threatening challenge, but I would be happy to be wrong about this. I encourage you to chase your dreams. But chances are you don't need to be told or reminded to chase them if they're authentic. Kobe Bryant didn't wake up at twenty-one and say he wanted to be an NBA player. He had been playing basketball most of his life. Certain things are possible while others are difficult—not impossible. If you want to chase those dreams, all the power to you. For the rest of us, the sooner we come to terms with certain truths, the happier we will be. There's almost a checklist of things we need to come to terms with, so let's go over them.

#1 You're Having a Crisis

This doesn't mean you're a crazy person, and everyone's definition of a crisis is a little different. For some people, it consumes them daily and visibly affects their mood. For others, it's mostly internal, not shared with others. There is nothing wrong with either end of the spectrum; it's just important to note that you are struggling with some part of your current existence, and there is some form of confusion in your life, and you are searching for clarity.

There is a feeling in the middle of your chest every time you think of the future—this is what I mean by a crisis. It's not life threatening, and it doesn't cause cancer, but it's not great for your mental health or growth to go on ignoring it. Accept the confusion and allow yourself not to have the answers—you don't have to google anything. It's not important that you are currently on the path to the rest of your life, because as long as you are growing and learning as a person, you are OK. If you are not, then you have a platform for the work that needs to be done.

#2 The Grass Isn't Always Greener

Often when we find ourselves in times of trouble, we turn into escapists. We look for alternatives that are grossly distant from our current realities. The old fight-or-flight adage is very applicable here. So when we feel trapped, that feeling is shrouded with other intentions. We often tell ourselves we want to change cities to explore the world. We want to try another job because ours is holding us back. Our relationships are getting stiff, and we feel as if our lives are stagnant, and we don't want to wake up one day and be forty. Well, you're going to wake up one day and be forty. Unless you fall off the face of this planet or go all Benjamin Button on us.

It's important that we are always running toward something and not away from something. When we feel confused, the only answer may seem like a fresh start. This is not always the solution in life. We are often told never to make decisions in the darkness, and the same applies here. If you want to see the world or shift jobs, make sure it aligns with your values, and make sure it's for the right reasons. Running away from your problems won't solve them. It will only encourage them to follow you around and continue to bring you down. A change in scenery is only a temporary fix. A new job will become an old job after time. All things lose that appeal of new and shiny sooner or later, and the cycle repeats. By understanding and accepting your situation, you learn to beat the cycle.

#3 You Won't Be the Next

It's easy to see yourself doing a whole whack of things with your life. Media and the entertainment industry have done a fine job of making this seem possible. Alas, we must accept that certain things are not within our grasp.

I had a friend who loved to play hockey—naturally talented, born in a hockey town, and playing at a high level. Yet a time came when he needed to decide: Did he want to continue to spend eight hours a day passing the puck for a chance at the big show, sacrificing his youth and praying for no injury and his chance at payday? He examined the risk and went to a university and now has a wonderful life. He was strong enough to acknowledge his values and make a decision, and he hasn't looked back.

To some, that may sound like a tale of regret, but it's important to draw a bigger lesson. It's a story of courage and self-awareness. It's the strength to move forward in life and have the self-awareness to know it was the right call. Try to visualize whatever crazy dream you have in the back of your head. If you aren't already trying to make it happen for eight hours a day, you have two choices: start this second or quit. Be prepared to take risks, be ready to fail, be ready to make sacrifices, and always do what it takes to be number one. I believe it was Seth Godin who wrote a great book on quitting called *The Dip*—check it out; there is no shame in it.

Step Two: Cut the Shit, Social Media

Closer to the front of this handbook, I spoke about the effects that social media has on us and this whole quarter-life thing. We now understand that comparing our lives to the highlights of others only throws us deeper down the rabbit hole of a quarter-life crisis. In summation: Highlight-syndrome theory = social media = highlights. We digest social media daily, and it begins to blur our own reality.

Our new reality takes shape, and we expect our new situation to be full of highlights. However, when reality meets expectation, we are left with disappointment and a mean quarter-life crisis. So what? Are we to throw social media out the window and become Luddites? Am I preaching on my soapbox for you to throw away your television and only communicate through pigeon mail? Well, no, because then the world would be even more full of pigeon shit. I suggest that we cut down on the comparisons between our lives and others, and that starts with a culling of your social media profiles.

First, identify if you need to walk away from social media for a while. If most of the following circumstances are true, you should deactivate for some time.

- Any second you are alone, you are checking your phone for updates on social media apps.
- You check these apps even though there are no updates (mindless browsing).
- You've deleted a post/photo if it didn't receive an adequate number of likes.
- You have several selfies or have even hashtagged #YOLO (just a personal preference).
- You measure self-worth through your Facebook friends.
- You value others by the number of their following-to-follower's ratio.
- You get upset when people open your Snapchats but don't reply to texts.
- Without thinking, you type www.facebook.com into your browser as if it's a reflex.
- Your poops are lasting for twenty minutes (hemorrhoids, anyone?).

Here is my suggested prescription if you suffer from these symptoms. Delete all of these apps from your phone. This will stop you from mindlessly opening them. Any medium that sets unrealistic expectations in your life—cut it out. This is temporary and has two functions: (1) You need to learn to live life without your phone; and (2) you are no longer allowed to occupy your moments of alone time or silence with your screens. It will teach you to internalize more, reflect, think, and understand what being by yourself is all about.

In the process you will come to appreciate these moments. This isn't always easy, and our brains won't like it at first because we've hardwired them for Facebook digestion. A form of zombification takes hold when you use these platforms. The human system is based on finding optimizations (see metabolism), and it likes when it can slow down and do less—social media affords it that luxury, but it becomes dumber in the process. (Don't listen to me; I'm not a science guy.)

Personally, I try to experiment with large stints away from social media because I do exhibit some of those symptoms, and my system needs a reset once in a while. I recommend you start with one month. Try to deactivate Facebook; delete your apps for thirty days. See what kind of difference it makes. Observe differences in your communication patterns and how you interact with others. Try calling instead of texting your friends. In a world where most working skills are being eaten alive by technology, interpersonal communication is something that is becoming rapidly more and more important.

One month later

So you've managed to spend a month away from your apps—now what? You just reinstall them and go back to the same old song and dance? Nope. I have another exercise for you, if you are interested. Every day I want you to write down ten things you are grateful for in life— things that you love, things you wouldn't want to do without. I won't tell you what needs to go on the list. You can repeat the same things every day, but you can never look at any previous list you made.

Once the entire thirty days are done, you can review it all. This will teach you what things are important in your life and what is a priority. You will realize that maybe being a travel blogger isn't the best job for you because "being close to family" is something that came up during the thirty days in this self-observation exercise. Or your significant other is someone who kept popping up on the list; it's probably better that you don't take off for months at a time for work.

If you do this for thirty days, it will be easier to go back to social media and use it for its intended purpose. You will have a higher value for your own life, a better understanding of who you are as a person—and as a result you will be less prone to comparison. When you see other posts of highlights, you can be happy for your friends rather than green with envy. You will develop the ability to separate these posts as highlights rather than as everyday reality.

Disclaimer!

I will make an important point here—don't be shamed by your jealousy. You are allowed to be jealous since it is a human emotion, after all. We must accept our jealousy but not allow it to consume our thoughts and dictate our actions. We can't allow emotion to rule our lives and guide our decisions. You are allowed to get wanderlust while creeping your friends. Remember, we control our own emotions, and it is within our own power to be happy. Sidebar over.

After this, you will probably notice you will use and frequent your social media a little less. It won't be your gut instinct to click on that app because you will be more focused. I can't promise you there is one absolute solution in this regard. Getting over this hump takes a lot of work and time, and it doesn't happen overnight. But as you work on yourself as a person, every day gets better and better, and color starts to come back to your life. Without thinking, the things that never held any real value in your life will start shrinking, and the beautiful things will start blossoming and becoming clearer.

The last challenge I have in the social media step is whenever you are feeling angst, jealousy, or a slight feeling of worthlessness, you should write about it. Write 250 words. Just put whatever is going on in your head on a piece of paper. It's important that you get that negativity out of your head and keep it from occupying your working memory. Getting those words out will help give you clarity and the ability to see these thoughts for what they really are—just thoughts—ideas not meant to rule your being.

So, in summary, it's important to take a step back, reflect, and observe. I'm not forcing this step down your throat. It has no scientific proof. It is just something that I have used myself and some friends have used to help them down a path.

Step Three: Build Yourself

This isn't an obscure *RoboCop* reference. I am not asking you to get robot legs, and don't even google robot legs. I am referring to bettering yourself as a person. One of the reasons we so easily fall victim to a quarter-life crisis is that we aren't well equipped to deal with it. We are often missing a sense of self. I believe there are three key elements in building yourself as a person: self-esteem, character, and self-investment.

People often believe that they have great levels of self-esteem. I'm using myself as an example here. I often confuse self-esteem for self-confidence. Believe it or not, they are two very different things. Self-confidence is a feeling of trust in one's abilities, qualities, and judgment. Self-esteem reflects a person's overall subjective emotional evaluation of his or her own worth. It is a judgment of oneself as well as an attitude toward the *self*.

They are two very different things, and it is easy to have one without the other. I can be confident in many things. I can believe I am doing well with my schoolwork or great at my full-time job, and it's very helpful that these institutions lay out performance benchmarks to compare myself against.

Before I go deeper down this rabbit hole, I want to make a point. I am not a certified anything. These are my observations and learning through my own experiences.

Self-esteem comes from the inside. There are no performance metrics for it; it's difficult to quantify. I've noticed that performance metrics are a one-way street for self-esteem. If you do well and overachieve, you can boost your self-confidence but not impact your self-esteem. However, a poor performance can affect both negatively.

So how does this relate to a quarter-life crisis? A part of this crisis comes from a poor evaluation of yourself. You diminish your worth when you shouldn't. Because of the confusion in your life, you believe that you are often the problem, and you tell yourself it's your fault for feeling this. It gets worse because you might believe that you are a special flower and no one else gets how you are feeling. But when you understand you aren't alone and you can accept this confusion, you can start on the next two steps.

Invest in Your Personal Stock Market

Think of yourself as a long-term stock. You are not a penny stock. You don't get to buy low, wait a couple of days to make a couple of bucks, and cash out. We are safe investments with a low risk and high reward, but you have to put in the time and attention. You have to continue to invest over time and be patient, and eventually that investment will pay dividends. Payoffs include boosts in self-esteem and advances in your career, relationships, and even your finances.

So where do you register for your GHIC (General Human Investment Certificate)? Well, there's good news: you don't need any capital to start. That list of things you are so grateful for in life will be your initial investment. Now, all of the work you do will be centralized around that list.

Here's an example: Remember the football player? He

determined that football was important in his life as it kept occurring on his list. Everything he began to do started to support that. He stayed in shape, developed his physical health, and continued to raise his football IQ. He still studied through online university resources to stay sharp. He studied game film and reached out to old football coaches for mentoring, which turned into his coaching opportunity. He didn't have a lot of spare time, but having a lot of spare time wasn't on his list of things he was grateful for.

His GHIC was paying off in dividends. He continued to learn and grow, and as a result he continued to achieve. In order to do well on this new form of stock exchange, here's a summary:

- Identify the things that are fulfilling to you and you want to improve on.
- Continue to learn and grow as a person.
- Set short-, mid-, and long-term goals.
- Focus on these tasks, and you will see your crisis get less and less intense

Building Character

I spoke about character earlier in this handbook, when we talked about the difference between character and values. Rather than repeating that, I figured I would give you a case study of the effects that a strong character has.

My friend the football player struggled for a long time before he found his path. Adversity was a constant, and he was disappointed everywhere he turned. My friend was confident he would get a spot in the draft. He knew he wanted to play in the NFL one day. His name was never called. He woke up at 5:00 a.m. after the draft was done and worked out for what I was told was the entire day. The days went by, and he would stare at his phone as if he were waiting for a girl to text him back.

Still, nothing. He began to lose hope with only a couple of weeks until the official kickoff of NFL training camps. He kept training, kept staying in shape, day after day. Finally, he was brought in to try out for the fifty-two-man roster for one team. He worked his ass off day in and day out throughout training camp. He deserved to make that roster, but I guess politics got in the way. It's not my job to speculate. He was cut but told he would get a call for the practice squad. The team kept that promise, but he would spend the next two months bouncing around practice squads, never really getting a shot at playing.

Finally, the calls stopped coming. However, my friend never gave up. That's part of his character. When adversity came knocking, he trained harder and gave it his all. Even when his quarter-life crisis smacked him in the face, he kept on training. The harder he worked, and the smarter he worked, the more doors started opening up. His coaching position in football organically grew out of his goals to get into the NFL. Had he not kept training, he would never have reached out for training and football advice and never would have landed that coaching job.

The point I'm making with this example is how character got someone through a very tough situation. Character is that moral compass that keeps you from straying from your partner when temptation is the worst; it's the ability to tell that person no thanks for the drink and head on home. Character is how you react when it's Friday at four and your boss piles a bunch of work on your desk. Character is taking the time to tailor your résumé and make that cover letter kick-ass before submitting it after being rejected the last forty times.

Character also isn't something that just appears. You must build it. If you have a strong and positive character, a quarter-life crisis begins to get smaller and smaller. The angst becomes trivial, and you begin to trust yourself as you move forward. This is about deciding who it is you want to be. You don't have to decide your profession or your career for the next twenty years. Trust me—for people our age, this is not the most important thing. Our paths in an era of constant transformation will most likely change several times. Don't believe me? Technology in the last ten years has moved a hundred times faster than in the last one hundred years, and it will continue to do so, and the entire job market will continue to shift.

Instead of worrying about keeping up with the change, decide on the type of person you want to be. How will you treat others? How will you treat yourself? Are you going to be able to push yourself to get up at 5:00 a.m. to start the day early? Are you going to have the determination to get it done, to push through when you've been beaten down? I can't give you character, or a step-by-step guide on how to build it (at least not in this book), but I can tell you that you must simply start. You've got to believe in something. That brings me to our last step.

Step Four: Believe in Something

I think golf is one of the most fascinating sports/activities/hobbies (whatever you want to call it, I'm not getting into the argument of what defines a sport). Most sports involve a sense of mastery. Seeing a master at work is a beautiful thing, whether it's making that free kick right around the wall in soccer, nabbing that incredible catch, or executing that perfect spiral. However, golf is an imperfect sport. No one has mastered golf. Every shot has to be different, and more than any other sport, the mental game is enough to completely throw off your entire round.

You can be golfing extremely well, and then one bad shot can ruin your entire round. You begin each hole thinking about that bad swing, then performing that bad swing, duffing the ball, and throwing your pitching wedge onto the green. I've played rounds of golf where it was impossible to get out of this rut, and I went from playing decently (for me) to not being able to hit the ball. I got in my own head and didn't believe I could get it done. I lost trust in my own swing.

Life is a lot like this. If you don't believe in something, then you stand for nothing. I can't tell you what to believe in. A lot of people believe in religion, a higher power, themselves, or a set of rules. They have a fundamental belief and a set of guiding principles that steer them through life. Character is how you react, whereas your beliefs are why you react. It was my friend's character that got him out of bed every morning, but it was his belief that he could accomplish this and the belief that he belonged in football that tell why. Whether or not that ever came to fruition, he had to keep believing in that.

Your beliefs give you purpose, give you meaning—that's the stuff you are looking for, isn't it? I mean, isn't that what you've been looking for in this entire quarter-life crisis? What makes you think you'll find meaning in another city or another job?

Let's take a gander at the universe for a quick second. It's massive, go to Carl Sagan for a second; in the grand scheme of things, we are specs of dust. Meaning is a pretty big thing, and meaning of life is something even bigger. To believe that we will find this meaning in a geographic or occupational change is ridiculous.

I've had people ask me what to believe in—whether it be a religion or whatever. Whenever people ask me about religion (although I am in no way, shape, or form qualified to answer the question), I answer that one should go with whichever one you were raised with. Everyone tries to accomplish the same thing, when you look at it. People try to build themselves into moral and kind people who do good for themselves and others around them. Their beliefs give them meaning. So when the questions come, the answers are there.

If you have meaning, the questions become easier to answer. Why am I training? Because I believe I will be an NFL player. Why am I staying loyal to my spouse? Because I believe in fidelity. Why am I not out binge drinking every night? Because I believe that everything is good in moderation.

What I am saying is sounding like a broken record. You

just have to believe in something. Hopefully, it's something that makes you a better person. Perhaps it makes you a moral, contributing member of society—just not another person who forgets to use a blinker and shifts into the next lane, forcing another driver to slam on the brakes. We have enough of those people; we don't need any more. If your belief is to not be one of those people, you've in fact immediately added benefit to the world we live in and made it a better place, so thank you.

Your beliefs will be what get you through the tough times of this crisis. When that noonday devil comes creeping into your life and you begin to question why, you'll have the answer.

Remember my travel writer friend? Well, she's good at what she does. She starts every single day with one hour of straight, mundane writing. She works on her sentence structure, grammar, and syntax, and she follows this up every day with another hour of just creative writing.

Every day she repeats this process. It's dull, it's boring, and you can bet your ass through the course of it she asks herself why she is bothering to do this. Where is the meaning in this repetition? But she remembers her beliefs, and suddenly that creeping-crisis feeling crawling up her leg (she double-checks to make sure it's not a spider) starts to fade away. Her belief is that in order to be a successful writer, she must master her craft. She believes that this is what a master of a craft does— practices and practices and practices. She believes that this will lead to her success, so she understands that process, takes a breath, grabs a coffee, and gets back to work.

This isn't just applicable with mastery; it's applicable in our daily lives. You can apply this concept to your gym routine, to your nine-to-five job, and to your wine-sniffing class. It's that class you are taking so you aren't so embarrassed when you go on a date and need to pick out a wine, with that whole smell and taste routine, and your date thinks you're really cultured and wants to go on a second date.

I'm saying there is beauty to be found in the daily grind. There is beauty to be found in the lack of one. It's about acknowledging it. Every day can be different, but some things must be the same. A great golf swing is a consistent and repeating golf swing. Think Tom Brady throws the ball differently every time? No, it's the same throw each time he hucks it.

The old quote that I love, however, is now overused, overquoted, and has been turned to rubbish. It is the one that speaks to greatness as a habit. Remember that next time you think you need a change in your life. Trust in your beliefs, and if you don't have any, start to build them.

CHAPTER 8

COFFEE IS FOR CLOSERS

I'm throwing a lot of things at you—I understand this, and it's going to take some time to digest. Don't be so concerned that you are turning twenty-five in a couple of months. Why is twenty-five this magic number people have? Why is it so scary? Every time I have another friend turning twenty-five, I hear some sob story about how they are getting old. Why does twenty-five have to be such a big deal? Why is this a milestone in our lives, and who made these rules?

It has been fairly common to have a milestone every three years or so. At five years old, we started school. In between five and ten, some religious celebrations or a mini graduation was held. Ten years old was a decade old, so that was a huge deal. At thirteen you became a stuck-up brat. After that was your sweet-sixteen birthday, then high school graduation and college graduation. And then? You turn twenty-five. You're looking for a milestone, but there doesn't seem to be one in sight. Why aren't people celebrating my existence? Didn't I do something that warrants a Dairy Queen cake? Where are the gowns?

It would seem to me that twenty-five is just some made-up number that we decide to place emphasis on. We make it out to be a negative age. You're now on the wrong side of your twenties marching slowly toward the Rapture or something.

At the end of the day, all that advice I just gave you, all of those steps, and understanding all of the causes of this may not even help you if you can't accept this. It's up to you to decide the type of person you want to be. So remember, before I start to wrap this handbook up, twenty-five is nothing but a number—it should serve as a reminder of the awesome life you've led so far, the gifts you've been given, and maybe even a starting point for something new, but it shouldn't be looked at as a negative. I mean, after all, twenty-five is an awesome age. Now I can totally rent a car, so nothing is standing in my way of global domination.

Wrapping Up

We've been on a pretty crazy journey. Some of the bits of advice I have written may have resonated with you, stuck with you—others, not so much. Some of the things may have caused you to be thrown deeper down the well of your crisis, causing you to think more and more about your future. Some points I've made might have given you a little bit of relief. This handbook, like life, is really what you make of it.

I've done my best to detail what the problems are (at least in my own eyes) and have tried to help you find solutions to them. My solutions aren't the gospel, and there are other steps to success. The steps I have given you are mostly ones that have helped me—and others. There isn't only one way of doing things.

You may have read this, followed the steps, and still not have gotten all of the answers. Well, as crazy as I still sound—that's part of life, and it's awesome.

There's something fun about not knowing how something will turn out. You get mad when someone spoils a television show for you, but how about if someone spoiled something with a little more weight, like life? Sure, it would be interesting to look into a crystal ball and see what the future holds, but that's not what living is. We never know what's coming next. We never know what the next moment in our life will bring. We can only enjoy the one we are in now. I'll give you one final example of this, but this time it's about me.

I used to think a lot of different things. My mind on any given day is a lot like scrambled eggs. I used to believe that life was a collection of experiences, and at the end of the day, that's what I lived for. I used to say that I needed to experience new things. There was still so much for me to experience in my twenties, and there was still so much of the world I had left to explore. I would think all these things, and then I would always get upset. There is no life in seeking out experience. Life is found in the right now, and we can never forget that.

Part of being a twentysomething is confusion, existential angst, and feeling meaningless, as if we are alone in the world or lost. Part of being twentysomething is thinking no one will love us and regretting something but learning from it. We aren't supposed to have all the answers; we are only in our twenties, after all. It's when we embrace that unknown that it starts to get a little bit better. It's when we acknowledge that we don't know what comes next that we can begin to smile and begin to enjoy the moments of blissful ignorance, but wonderful growth.

We can never know what comes next, but we can be prepared for it. We can never see what's around the corner, but we can build ourselves as people to be ready for whatever is there, and that building process might end up guiding our path. The truth of the matter is that you aren't alone. There are millions of others just like you. We are all lost; we are all wanderers in our own mind. There is beauty to be found in this. You just have to open your eyes to it and accept it.

Don't look for affirmation in social media or from others; let it come from within you. Never forget that you are awesome. Never let a post, picture, or number of likes take that away from you. You are great in your own way, so screw whatever anyone else says. You don't need anyone's opinion but your own, so go for the gusto, do you, be the best person you can be. Being a twentysomething and going through this quarter-life crisis is a crazy adventure. We can either sulk through it, ignore it, or realize its existence and ride the wave. You don't have to "find" yourself. But at least look around. I'm not going to spoil it for you. You aren't going to find the answer, but you'll learn a lot about yourself in the process, and that's even better.

I wrote these pages not just for you, but for myself as well. You see, I too suffer from a quarter-life crisis. I turned twenty-five and felt all of these things. I've spent countless days on my parents' couch talking about my meaning in life, my contribution to the world, and what my purpose was. Trust me. I have been there. As words filled these pages, I have found comfort in my own situation and learned more about myself in the process.

With that being said, if these pages help one person, or if they make people smile or laugh, or if they give them comfort—it was all worth it. All the hours involved were well spent.

Thanks for reading. I wish you the best on your journey. May it be filled with beauty, wonderful experiences, awesome people, and plenty of learning.

ABOUT THE AUTHOR

Matt Topic has always worn many hats. Between his service in the army, his time as a Starbucks Barista, a university student, radio show host, stand-up comedian, DJ, or working for the largest media company in Canada, he has amassed quite the collection. He draws on every experience, every encounter, and every relationship and channels them into this book.

Matt loves to spend his time with his guitar, on a surfboard, or behind the wheel of a car, always with a cup of coffee within arm's reach.

If you ever needed to look for him, he's likely be found on his Mom and Dad's patio, or somewhere near the ocean.

Made in the USA
San Bernardino, CA
17 December 2018